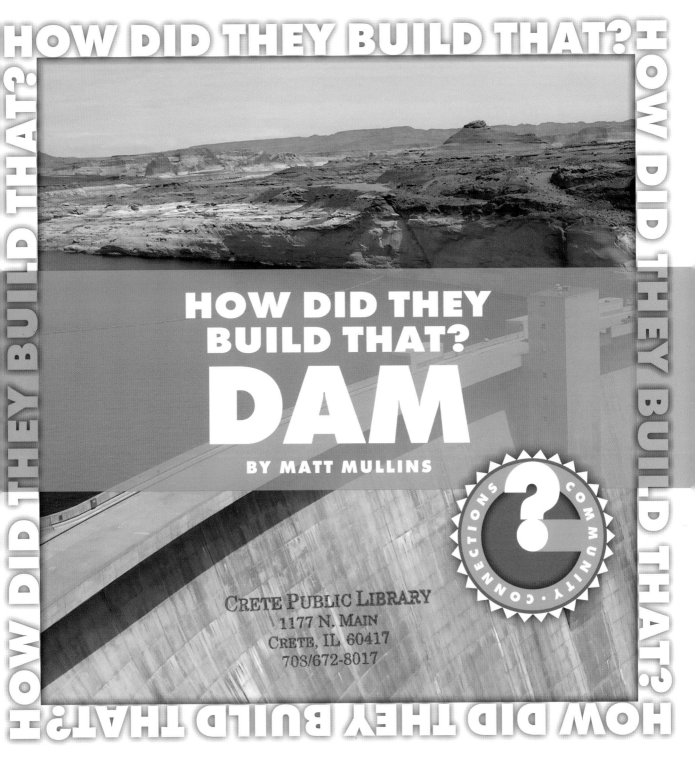

HOW DID THEY BUILD THAT?
DAM

BY MATT MULLINS

COMMUNITY · CONNECTIONS
?

Published in the United States of America by Cherry Lake Publishing
Ann Arbor, Michigan
www.cherrylakepublishing.com

Content Adviser: Nancy Kristof
Reading Adviser: Cecilia Minden-Cupp, PhD, Literacy Consultant

Photo Credits: Cover and page 1, ©Mary Lane, used under license from Shutterstock, Inc.;
page 5, ©iStockphoto.com/shmackyshmack; page 7, ©Bryan Busovicki, used under license
from Shutterstock, Inc.; page 9, ©iStockphoto.com/PeterAustin; page 11, ©iStockphoto.com/
asterix0597; page 13, ©Allen Furmanski, used under license from Shutterstock, Inc.; page 15,
©Robert McGouey/Alamy; page 17, ©iStockphoto.com/meltonmedia; page 19, ©mediacolor's/
Alamy; page 21, ©Lazar Mihai-Bogdan, used under license from Shutterstock, Inc.

LIBRARY OF CONGRESS CATALOGING-IN-PUBLICATION DATA
Mullins, Matt.
  How did they build that? Dam / by Matt Mullins.
    p. cm.—(Community connections)
  Includes index.
  ISBN-13: 978-1-60279-488-7
  ISBN-10: 1-60279-488-X
  1. Dams—Juvenile literature. I. Title. II. Series.
  TC540.M85 2009
  627'.8—dc22   2008046141

Cherry Lake Publishing would like to acknowledge the
work of The Partnership for 21st Century Skills. Please
visit www.21stcenturyskills.org for more information.

CONTENTS

HOW DID THEY BUILD THAT?

WHAT IS A DAM FOR?

Dams are huge **structures**. Some are very tall. Others are low and wide. Many are made of **concrete**.

Dams have different uses. Many are built to stop flooding. Others are built to make electricity.

Dams come in all shapes and sizes.

Many dams create a **reservoir**.
A reservoir looks like a big lake.
People can use these lakes for
boating, fishing, and swimming.
Reservoirs hold water that
is used for drinking or
watering crops.

Some dams are big enough for cars to
drive across.

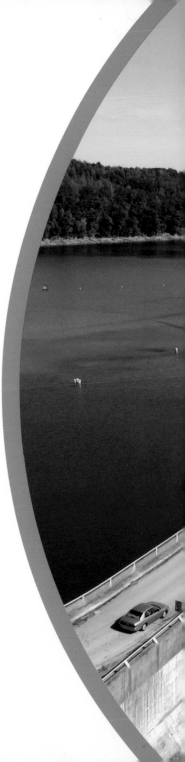

LOOK!

Look for pictures of three or four different dams. You will find some in books or online. How do the dams look the same? How are they different?

MOVING THE RIVER

Workers have been told to build
a dam. The dam will hold back
water from a river. Workers
have to move the river water
before they can build a dam.
If they don't, they will be
working in mud. A dam
needs a solid base to stand
on, not a muddy floor.

Workers must plan carefully before they start
building a dam.

How do workers move a river? They dig a long ditch or tunnel around the place where the dam will be built. This allows the river to flow around the work area. Workers remove the remaining water. Then they let the ground dry. This will be the **construction** site.

Construction vehicles can start working after the ground is dry.

Dig a small "river" in some soil. Fill it with water. Pick a spot where you would like to build a bridge. Dig a ditch or tunnel around that spot. Can you get water to flow around your construction site?

11

SEALING THE FLOOR

Workers dig out all the dirt and sand. Hard **bedrock** is left when the dirt and sand are gone. The bedrock gives the dam a strong base to stand on.

Hoover Dam is one of the largest dams in the world. Do you see the rock on the side of the dam?

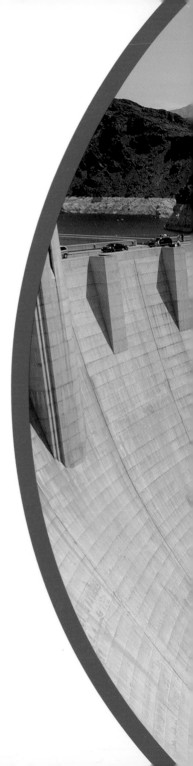

Most bedrock has cracks and holes in it. Crews seal these holes with a **cement** mixture. This creates a waterproof bottom for the dam. Now the rest of the dam can be built.

People aren't the only ones who build dams. This beaver is using mud to plug leaks in the dam it built.

When you visit a
dam, guess how
long it took to build.
Write down your
guess. Then go to
the library or search
online to find out how
long it took. Was
your guess correct?

15

BUILDING THE WALL

First, workers build **forms**. These wood walls are like empty boxes. Workers will fill these forms with wet concrete. Concrete is a mixture of cement, sand, gravel, and water. Concrete is very strong when it dries. Water cannot get through it.

Most dams are made of concrete.

Concrete is poured from giant buckets hanging on steel **cables**. Workers pour one layer and let it dry. Then they move the wood forms up and pour the next layer. They keep adding layers until the dam is finished. A tall dam can take a long time to build.

Many people and machines were needed to build China's Three Gorges Dam.

RELEASING THE RIVER

The dam is built. Workers let the river flow back to its regular path. Water builds up behind the dam wall. The water behind the wall forms the reservoir.

Now the dam is ready to do its work. Building a dam is a big job. Dams are big structures with big jobs to do!

Dams can create beautiful lakes, or reservoirs.

GLOSSARY

bedrock (BED-rok) solid rock below soil

cables (KAY-buhlz) thick wires or ropes

cement (suh-MENT) a gray powder made from crushed limestone that is mixed with water and left to dry until it hardens; one of the ingredients needed to make concrete

concrete (KON-kreet) material that hardens like stone and is made of cement, sand, gravel, and water

construction (kuhn-STRUHK-shuhn) having to do with building or making something

forms (FORMZ) wood frames that shape material

reservoir (REZ-ur-vwar) a place for collecting water

structures (STRUHK-churz) buildings or other things that are built

FIND OUT MORE

BOOKS

Murray, Julie. *Hoover Dam*. Edina, MN: ABDO Publishing, 2005.

Richards, Julie. *Dams*. North Mankato, MN: Smart Apple Media, 2003.

WEB SITES

Association of State Dam Safety Officials
www.damsafety.org/community/kids/?p=
0cefe3c0-b76d-432d-9d77-df304892e690
Learn more about dams and dam safety

Hoover Dam Factoids for Kids
www.usbr.gov/lc/hooverdam/educate/kidfacts.html
Fun facts about Hoover Dam from the U.S. Department of the Interior

TVA Kids: About Dams
www.tvakids.com/river/aboutdams.htm
Information from the Tennessee Valley Authority about dams and the power they provide

INDEX

24

ABOUT THE AUTHOR

Matt Mullins lives with his wife and son in Madison, Wisconsin. Formerly a journalist, Matt writes about science and engineering, current affairs, food and wine, and anything else that draws his interest.